IDAHO IS HOME

Fleeting Images, Personal Memories

To Justin,

*In good times, in bad times,
We'll be at your side forevermore.*

First Edition

Copyright © MCMXCIII United Clearinghouse Publishing
All rights reserved. No part of this book may be
reproduced in any form or by any electronic or mechanical
means, including information storage and retrieval systems,
without permission in writing from the publisher, except
by a reviewer who may quote brief passages in a review.
Manufactured in Hong Kong

Computer Architecture • Sally Schmelzer
Editor-In-Chief • Judd Golden
Photo/Journalist contributions • Barbara Pfeiffer • Jean Meyers • W. R. Wells • Olen Wood

Library of Congress Cataloging in Publication Data Pending

ISBN 0-9635209-9-7

Publisher: United Business Clearinghouse Publishing
P.O. Box 15001 Boise, Idaho 83715

Front Cover: Final moments of the day's sunlight settle on a Salmon River ranch.

INTRODUCTION

One out of every three residents of Idaho was born and raised in another part of the United States or another part of the world. What is Idaho's attraction?

Can you remember the personal circumstances that motivated you or your family to move to the Gem State? How would you compare the quality of life between Idaho and your former home? Was there a special person, a special place, a certain event or experience that caused you to fall in love with Idaho?

Through our editor contacts, these questions were distributed and made available to the people who lived and worked in the cities and small towns spottily distributed throughout Idaho. We made no restrictions as to how these stories ought to be written or presented, only that the information be factual.

The weeks and months passed, and slowly the reply envelopes began to trickle into our publishing offices in Boise. The stories were charming and quite interesting. The experiences which led to their migration to Idaho spoke with innocence and honesty, of hardships and humor regarding events, big and not so big, that occurred long ago as well as quite recently.

Why did one-third of our state's population choose Idaho to be its new home? We genuinely wanted to know some of the answers to the questions of why, how, and when. After all, many people could have easily chosen the beautiful and sophisticated areas of California, Oregon, Washington, Wyoming, Utah, and Montana to call home. But, instead, they chose Idaho.

Granted, Idaho has been getting pretty good national press coverage lately from so many sources of information: skiing and hunting magazines, Audubon and wildflower clubs, wonderfully filmed nature programs on TV, the successes of local artists and writers, and so on.

We live within easy access to a beautiful and majestic part of the Northwest. Rivers run clean and cold. Large portions of mountain wildernesses are free of roads, but have thousands of miles of incomparable hiking trails. We have abundant prairies, alpine lakes, streams, and flowered meadowlands. Coyotes, deer, elk, bear, and bighorn sheep. Endless parks and reserves with mountain bluebirds and red-winged blackbirds. Migrating geese and pintail ducks that fill the moisture-laden skies in the spring and late autumn.

Nature's own personal network of miracles in this part of the world is not only bountiful, but accessible. Simply put on a pair of comfortable walking boots, grab the binoculars and a canteen filled with cold water, drive for a while in almost any direction, and enjoy some of the tucked-away treasures that await Idahoans 365 days of the year.

But what are the specifics, the details, the myriad decisions that lead individuals and families to pack up and move thousands of miles from their roots in Tennessee and Kentucky, Michigan and Wisconsin, New York and Delaware, Texas and California?

At a later date, our editor-in-chief decided to add another small series of questions to the ones mentioned earlier, in order to explore the thoughts and personalities of other Idaho residents from all around the state. We asked: If we could, somehow, bring some of America's favorite poets, artists, heroes, and heroines back to life, which ones would you invite to visit with you in Idaho? To what part of Idaho would you take them to visit? What would they have to say?

The reminiscences and answers to these questions are included in this book, and represent a cross section of the Idaho people: a young building contractor from Moscow, a school teacher from North Fork, a pioneer grandson from the Salmon River country, a financial consultant and retired shop owner from Boise, a World War II veteran from Juliaetta. Their generosity in sharing their tales with us may help, in a small way, to coalesce native and non-native Idahoans. We all share one common trait, and that is our undying gratitude and affection for this wonderful part of the world that opened its doors and made so many of us feel "at home".

We offer you a sampling of the stories, the replies, and some of the personal photographs that have been sent to us, along with my sincere thanks to those "homegrown" Idahoans who have given so many of us a chance to prove our worth, build our homes, and raise our kids.

Walter Wells
Chief Executive Officer
United Business Clearinghouse Publishing

MIGRATION OF THE STRODES

The Strodes came to Idaho quite a long time ago. The family has lived in Idaho some 38 years before statehood, so as a fourth generation Idahoan, I'd like to relate a few of the reasons as to how and why we came to settle here.

Let me first tell you a bit of the family history and so on. The Strodes migrated to America from England sometime during the early 1600's. They settled for a while in what is now West Virginia and later moved to Bourbon County, Kentucky. There they built Strodes' Fort on Strodes' Creek, where they, off and on, fought Indians. They next turned up around Cook County, Tennessee, where in 1833 my great grandfather, John Strode, was born.

At age 19, John headed west for Idaho Territory herding an ox team pulling his covered wagon. He was reputed to have walked much of the distance to Boise Valley in order to better drive his ox team.

If my great grandfather could be here today to talk about when his affection for this new Idaho Territory began in earnest, I feel certain he would not talk about the pretty eyes and face of a young pioneer girl, or the sight of a full harvest moon over the Sawtooths, or a field of colorful wildflowers on a spring morning.

Although he undoubtedly enjoyed many of these pleasant experiences, I feel he would, instead, talk to us about a particular stone he uncovered one day while doing a little prospecting in a creek bed located between Atlanta and Rocky Bar. This discovery assayed out to be worth over $3,000. At that time, during the mid 1860's, gold was worth some $16 - $17 an ounce. Do a little arithmetic and you'll appreciate the huge size that single nugget must have been. And I'm not exactly sure what this much money meant 125 years ago to a young man, but I do know $3,000 meant a heck of a lot more back then than it does today. This large sum of money helped to start the family out in the livestock business, where they remained for well over 100 years.

During the late 1890's and early 1900's, John Strode and Sons owned a ranch on Boise property that is now the area around 16th and 17th Streets, home of Joe Albertson's original store. State Street was then known as Valley Road, and Boise City was a whole mile away around the area of First to Sixth Streets. A brick building still stands on 16th or 17th Street that was one of the residence buildings on the ranch. It is now an attorney's office, I believe. John Strode is buried in the pioneer section of Morris Hill Cemetery in Boise.

As for myself, at an early age I drifted up to the Salmon River country of Idaho where I remain to this day and intend to remain always! I probably know the Salmon River country as well as anyone alive today, having lived at Clayton, Challis, Salmon City, North Fork, Gibbonsville, Riggins, White Bird, Yellow Pine, and Thunder Mountain. In my Idaho travels I have journeyed over much of it by foot, horseback, automobile, boat, and airplane. I sincerely love every square inch of it!

My time and energy spent exploring and enjoying the many facets of the Salmon River area did not result in high financial rewards. But I've always believed, "It is not he who has little and is happy, only he who has little and desires much, who is poor."

David L. Strode, North Fork

State and federally protected rivers and streams near Henry's Lake satisfy the thirst of moss-covered trees and fragile summer flowers.

"I would enjoy being with William Clark and Meriwether Lewis as they re-crossed the Northern mountains of Idaho. Only this time, they would be traveling with a little more comfort and style. Meriwether would be at the wheel of a high-powered luxury Lexus on Interstate 90, traveling east to west at about 75 MPH. Bill Clark would be adjusting the Willie Nelson songs on the tape deck. Would they be inclined to discuss the improvements in being able to take a smooth four-lane expressway compared to carrying those awkward canoes over the Lolo Pass, or would their conversation center around stopping into the next Pancake House or drive-thru McDonalds Restaurant for a couple of burgers and shakes?"

John Pack, Lewiston

Deserted one-room schoolhouse nestles on a hilltop near the Salmon River.

Posing for a photograph is a big attraction for folks who appreciate the long network of split-log fences that stretch in all directions from the town of Stanley.

PARTNERSHIP WITH THE MOUNTAINS

"I would like a ticket to Victor, Idaho," I told an agent at Grand Central railroad station in New York City.

The agent rummaged through several books on his counter. Then he left the window, consulted with a man at the back of the room, disappeared behind a steel rack, and came back to the window.

"WHERE did you say you wanted to go?" he asked, with a trace of irritation in his voice.

"Victor, Idaho."

He then headed for the back of the room again whereupon I heard impatient murmurings on the long line in back of me. New Yorkers usually take waiting in line in stride. However, when the line stalls, tempers flare.

Evidently very few inhabitants of this great metropolis ever ventured to Victor, Idaho. Finally, however, the station agent found my ticket. "Send me a potato," he said as I left.

In June of 1948 I rode coach to the end of a branch line of the Union Pacific and stepped off the train for my first glimpse of Idaho. More memorable to me, though, than the panoramic view was the perfumed air. Clean, dry, pine-wafted, mountain-cooled, invigorating, fresh air! I didn't sniff it; I DRANK IT.

That year I stayed in Idaho just long enough for the bus ride across the border to Wyoming where I spent the summer climbing the peaks of the Grand Tetons.

In the fall of 1948 I returned to my teaching job in Manhattan, thankful I could escape the city during the summer heat when the skyscrapers became vertical ovens. In other ways, too, my life was better than that of the average urbanite.

The apartment I rented, half a block from the Delancey Street police precinct station granted protection even when I came home late at night. A friend had installed burglar-proof locks on my door and windows.

My landlady in New York, an elderly Jewish woman who lived directly across the hall from me, kept the five-story building immaculately clean. Many a morning I met her scrubbing the hall steps on her hands and knees. On Friday mornings she baked and cooked, often saving batches of this delicious food for me.

She insisted that tenants keep the downstairs door locked so that strangers couldn't wander through the building. A good neighbor six days a week, she did not, however, tolerate anyone ringing her doorbell on Saturdays.

"Bei mir iss Shabbash (This is my Sabbath!)," she hollered, slamming the door on anyone who disturbed her holy day.

Since Mrs. Pollock was illiterate, I returned her favors by reading her mail to her, and occasionally writing out a birthday card for a relative.

I enjoyed my job on the upper west side of Manhattan as a tenured elementary school teacher. The school housed about 50 classes, grades one through six. Eighty percent of the children were black, five percent were Puerto Ricans, and the other fifteen percent represented every race, nationality, and creed....a diversity that I found fascinating.

In those days new teachers were usually assigned to schools in poor neighborhoods. After three years, when they achieved tenure, most would apply for a transfer to a "better" neighborhood. When a teacher opted to stay at a school, however, the parents, especially the black parents, were extremely grateful. They realized that education was the vital key to an improved status. Thus, although the work was difficult, I felt appreciated. The media constantly focused on the troubled youths who came into conflict with the law. I marveled at how many of the youngsters succeeded in circumventing their poverty with heroic and meaningful lives.

On school days I could always get a seat on the subway riding uptown against the main flood of workers traveling downtown. Nor did I need to hold my high heel in readiness to dig into the foot of a possible pervert getting too friendly in an overcrowded car. My mother lived in a west side apartment so that on nights when I had to attend PTA meetings I could take a bus to her place rather than risk a night ride on the subway.

Thus I had made the necessary adjustments to survive in this mega-township. What always amazed me was that this community of 8 million inhabitants actually could, and did, function. People worked, children grew up. Heat....power....transportation....entertainment etc. were available. Garbage was collected (well, most of the time). And there was always the opportunity for me to leave the city every summer.

And leave I did, for Cape Breton in Nova Scotia, the newly opened Alaska highway, the Gore Range in Colorado, the Berkshire Hills in Massachusetts, and Nantucket Island. An army knapsack loaded with 60 pounds of camping gear supplied my summer needs. Each year I found it harder and harder to return to New York. In 1951 I made my first break from Manhattan to teach in the tundra village of Kasigluk, Alaska.

After a year on Eskimo time, in which "right away" could mean next week and "soon" could mean within a year, I could not readjust to New York City's pace. My friends couldn't understand why I never ran to catch a bus. They frowned when I elected to wait on the curb for the light to change rather than dodge the traffic to cross the street a few seconds sooner.

At the age of 30, after many vagabond summers, I began to dream about settling down, getting married, and having some children of my own. I had enjoyed my childhood on New York City pavements roller skating and playing hopscotch, stoop ball, and, of course, double dutch. Skinned knees and a spanking for wearing out my shoes too fast were the only dangers I faced. I could understand why parents now refuse to let their 10-year-old children play outside by themselves, yet I also felt that it was equally dangerous to a child's welfare to be raised with this degree of overprotection.

Furthermore, attractive as domesticity was beginning to appear, I sincerely dreaded marrying into a humdrum existence. The men I met in New York lacked a sense of adventure. I resolved to exercise my nesting instincts elsewhere.

After a bout with pneumonia during the winter of 1955, I remembered the invigorating western air I first breathed in Victor, Idaho. Many evenings I mused over the map of Idaho; the national forests and primitive areas beckoned me. I sang over and over:

> In a mountain greenery
> where God paints the scenery
> just two crazy people together.

One morning as I arrived at school already stressed out from the ride on the screechy, smelly, dirty subway, I asked myself seriously if that was what I wanted to look forward to for the next 35 years.

When July finally came, I flew to Idaho Falls. From there I rode a bus to Salmon and hopped on mail stages to Challis and Sunbeam Dam where I decided to camp for a few weeks. I thought how nice it would be to establish a homestead on the beautiful Salmon River!

At Sunbeam I experienced my first Idaho acculturation as I made friendly small talk mingling with the fisherman perched on the dam. I asked one fisherman who was struggling to keep his footing as he hauled in a fish, "Doesn't anyone ever fall off?"

"No, but they sometimes get pushed off," he growled as other die-hard fisherman glared at me in agreement.

That ended my friendly small talk with anyone attached to a fishing pole. Idahoans not attached to fishing poles were more hospitable. They invited me to join them for hikes, campfire gatherings, swims at Stanley Hot Springs, and charming trips to Sun Valley.

After exploring the Yankee Fork vicinity, I transported my little mountain tent to Redfish Lake for another four weeks of outdoor recreation. Here I made more friends, among them a family from Salmon. When I spouted forth about the beauties of the Sawtooth Mountains and confessed my yearnings about a possible move to Idaho, they suggested I check at the Statehouse in Boise for teacher vacancies in the state.

A caretaker at the campground arranged a ride for me with a guest at Redfish Lodge who was driving to Boise that week over Lowman, which at that time was a narrow, dirt road. Clouds of dust floated off my gear and my skirt when he dropped me off at a hotel lobby in Boise.

At the Statehouse, I was told of a vacancy in a one-room school with five pupils, in Goldburg, in the Challis school district. A telephone call granted me an interview. I loved the smell of the newly mown hay on the trip back to Challis. The superintendent probably didn't believe my credentials, however, for he did not hire me. I swam off my frustration in the Challis Hot Springs. As a last resort, I decided that since Salmon wasn't too far away, I would apply there for a position. I did not want to endure another year in New York City. Not one more year.

The Salmon superintendent had no openings in the city, but he told of a vacancy in Cobalt, a small mining town in the Salmon National Forest. Since I was able to give the Salmon family I previously met at Redfish Lake as a reference, this superintendent was willing to consider me for the job.

Not having a car, I started to walk towards Cobalt, certain that even though the road had light traffic, I would hopefully meet a vehicle of some sort sooner or later. I couldn't honestly define the way into the mountains as a road, but it was the route everyone traveled. Luckily, the milk truck came by soon to spend the day in Cobalt, giving me a chance to explore the town and guaranteeing me a ride back to Salmon in the late afternoon. Even luckier, the driver of the milk truck was on the Salmon school board.

During that unforgettable summer so long ago, I remember looking at Idaho with the eyes of a transient tourist, enamored only of its scenic vistas and recreational offerings. But now, strolling down Cobalt's main street, I began to see the human drama of people in partnership with the mountains. I saw the harsher side of these hills as miners were turning into their gates bone weary from working their shifts deep underground. Yet I sensed that despite the

Daisies straddle a wire fence.

Treasured, active churches dot the small, charming towns of rural Idaho. This is the community church in Ola.

The basics of family farming are learned early in the lives of Idaho youngsters.

demands this rugged and lovely land made on its people, it also rewarded their struggles with a serenity and fortitude that city people lacked.

Taking a last look at Cobalt as I climbed into the milk truck for the return trip, I realized I had fallen in love with more than a place; I had fallen in love with a way of life. I knew I wanted very much to be more than an Idaho spectator. I didn't merely want to live in Idaho; I wanted to become a bona fide Idahoan.

When we entered Cobalt, crossing an old rickety wooden bridge spanning Panther Creek, it was love at first sight. A self-contained village at an elevation of 5,000 feet, it was completely surrounded by wilderness and canopied with a blue, blue sky....what a paradise! I couldn't believe that a community could function in this remote isolation. It was as much of a marvel to me as the millions of people who were coexisting on the island of Manhattan. The people were extremely friendly, stopping their yard work to chat, inviting me into their homes for coffee. The school seemed to be a good facility with windows offering a grand view of the steep Idaho mountain slopes. My heart sang:

> In a mountain greenery
> where God paints the scenery

Halfway back to Salmon, the milk truck driver stopped to visit with a weathered prospector, who was traveling in the same direction. It was suggested that I transfer to the prospector's pickup since he would be getting to Salmon much sooner.

"She's OK. She's a school teacher." I overheard the milk truck driver tell the prospector. I, however, was not given any assurance that the prospector was OK.

But he was. In fact, he was terrific. He conducted a guided tour all the way back to Salmon. "Over there," he said, "you climb them hills up and you look the meadow down and that is where the elks live."

Relating tales of his prospecting ventures, he told of the advice he gave his buddy as they were sitting around a campfire one evening: "Every living thing is good for something. EVEN YOU, JOHN."

Back in the town of Salmon, even though it meant a huge salary cut, I told the superintendent I would accept the teaching position. After I signed the contract he said, "Well, well, well. New York City to Panther Creek. That could be some adjustment."

Now I had just enough time to return to New York, arrange for my household goods to be shipped to Cobalt (with a prayer that the New York moving company would eventually be able to find this little town), and fly back to Idaho for the opening of the school term.

In choosing to move to Idaho, I felt I had made a Goldilocks decision. Alaska was so cold. Wyoming was so windy. Idaho was JUST RIGHT.

The Calera Mining Company in Idaho rented me a partially furnished apartment which served me until my own furniture arrived....many weeks later. The movers eventually DID find Cobalt. As providence would have it, my apartment faced the single men's dormitory.

It wasn't long before I met Glenn, a geologist, who enjoyed doing useful things such as hunting, fishing, and prospecting. Glenn was a transplant lured away from Nevada's dry stretches by Idaho's rushing streams. In March of that year, when ice still covered the steelhead holes, when the hillsides were still snow covered to hinder good prospecting, and when the hunting season was closed, we were married.

Later, when the Cobalt mine closed, we moved to a uranium mine in Wyoming, but not before we bought ourselves 113 acres of Idaho, right on the Salmon River at Kriley Gulch, in hope that we could one day return. The land was mostly a rocky, sagebrush hillside, and the taxes in the early 1960's were only $9 yearly. Our nearest neighbor in any direction was a mile distant.

We returned in 1971 with a young family of two children. Our hands bore the blisters and callouses attesting to the hard work of establishing a homestead where as yet there was no power, no sewers, no fences, not even a creditable road. But we were where we both wanted to be, back in Idaho.

Our children grew up as ridge runners, claiming the territory from our home to the Montana border as their backyard. They learned how to cope with rattlesnakes, coyotes, porcupines, bears, and weasels that often tried to steal fish from their creels. Our son earned teen spending money by haying, tree planting, logging, and wrestling down calves for branding. Our daughter was equally competent, slinging a gun over her shoulder to bag and gut out her deer, at the same time sewing her own gowns for the school dances.

I loved what Idaho did for my children even more than what it did for me. Yet I don't fret because they left the state to establish homes and careers of their own. I don't think we should be so insular-minded that we regret the exodus of our best young people to other states. We are, after all, one country, regardless of which state we live in. In fact, I think our young people will have a wholesome, salutary effect on communities outside of Idaho. The delicious fresh air they breathed for many years undoubtedly nourished their brain cells enabling them to bring fresh insights to the problems all communities face, and to bring an infusion of vitality to their new friends and new neighborhoods.

I say this not just because of my own children. Having taught school in Lemhi County for fifteen years, I've noticed that our Idaho youngsters do very well wherever they go, in whatever fields of occupation they choose. They are Idaho's best advertisement.

Did I ever miss New York City? Occasionally I longed for a swim in the Atlantic and a walk along the beach on a summer afternoon. At times I missed the masses of interesting people, the cosmopolitan melting pot.

I wish I could have celebrated with my old New York landlady when I read about her heroism in the *GRIT* newspaper. Two men were dumb enough to break into her apartment on the day she was preparing for her Shabbash. She foiled their robbery attempt by throwing hot chicken soup in their faces.

Some people, however, like my mother, would never leave New York City. She lived in an apartment with an incinerator belching out pollution continuously right outside her bedroom window. She stayed there to gasp out her last days worrying about the rattlesnakes on our property out in Idaho.

On my last visit to New York, I was approaching a corner bus stop en route to the airline terminal building in midtown. I clutched my purse even tighter than usual, for I realized that lugging a heavy suitcase made me especially vulnerable. Walking down a New York City street, even in broad daylight, is like playing on a basketball court; you must be alert to every movement in front, in back, and on every side. I wasn't certain if my street smarts were still operative or if I was merely paranoid, but did that man suddenly change his course and start heading directly towards me? Luckily a cab cruised by, and instinctively I hailed it. "Got here just in time, didn't I?" the cab driver said. I couldn't wait to get back to Idaho.

Lotte K. Franklin, North Fork

Except for the chirping of a few mountain bluebirds, silence surrounds a home in the Elkhorn foothills.

What could be better than shooting a few games of eight-ball with Ernest Hemingway at some bar in Ketchum? What if he asked me when quail and chukar season opened? Would I have enough guts to ask him what he thought about those new $2,000,000 and $3,000,000 seasonal homes they're now building in areas where he used to fish for cutthroats and hunt for deer and elk?

After showing him some of these mega-homes and country ranches with the three car garages, suppose he insisted that I accompany him over to Whiskey Jacques' for a few bourbons and a couple of thick steaks, and we could discuss these newcomers from California? Just how, exactly, does one communicate with an American legend such as Ernie? It would be impossible, I'm sure, at least until I had a few rounds with him.

Jimmy Ross, Ketchum

The fabled ski slopes of Sun Valley are quiet and deserted, but they are a favorite summertime destination of hikers and photographers.

A darkening sky and falling aspen leaves remind residents in Sun Valley and Ketchum that hunting season can't be far away.

Redfish Lake is edged with a carpet of pine trees and morning fog while a fishing boat searches for the elusive coho salmon.

The foothills that surround Boise are mostly dry and brown during the summers, but the soft touch of the year's first snowfall is visible at the top.

HARVEST OF FIRE

The l950's brought the land draw to the Magic Valley, which is situated high on the Snake River plain in the middle of southern Idaho. The name is misleading as this is no valley, only acre after acre of dry, hard, rock-ridden flatland covered with sagebrush. Giving it away was virtually the last attempt by the state to settle the area. The "magic" would be for someone who could possibly make a living from that baked earth. This waterless wasteland barely supported rattlesnakes, coyotes, and jackrabbits. It was scorching hot in summer, freezing cold in winter, and the wind blew unceasingly.

The 1950's were also when Grandpa decided the "big money" was in sheep. We had sheep stalls, sheep chutes, sheep dip, sheep brands, sheep camps, sheepherders, sheep dogs, sheep shears, and sheep shit as far as the eye could see. We had shelter season, herding season, branding season, and lambing season. The only thing we didn't have was "money season."

Grandpa had an interesting sense of economics. About every five years or so he would predict financial success in a new area he was totally unprepared for. If it was dairy cows (mid 1970's) he would buy choice stock, build barns, put in milkers, set up pastures, and turn it all over to my father with the prediction that we were "sure to make a fortune." If it didn't pay off, and sometimes even if it did, he'd declare eventually, "I told you there wouldn't be any money in those damn cows. Beets! Sugar beets! That's where the big money is." So Grandpa would sell the cows and turn to buying tractors, plows, and planters. He'd section off the land and leave the empty barns with my father.

The "land draw" was not another scheme to make us rich. Grandpa put in his name and the names of each of his three sons so he could get as much land as possible to herd the sheep. They ended up drawing the driest of the dry, the dead volcano itself....the Kimama Butte. The butte was a miserable mound of rock and brush. We herded sheep out there only one year. The ones that weren't eaten by coyotes nearly starved on the sparse, yellow grass. Grandpa gave up on the sheep and the land in a hurry and resumed his search for "big money" closer to the river.

However, my father had finally been given something with his own name on it, and he saw it as more than just acres of dust and rock. It was his chance to finally come from behind, try to salvage the dreams of his dad, and begin his own vision of the future. He foresaw what irrigation could turn Idaho land into, and he began to work hard to pursue his dream of green, productive fields.

We started out with dry-land wheat, about 18 inches high where it grew at all. My brothers and I picked lava rock and put them in piles every 50 feet or so where the solid mounds of black stone had already erupted beneath the thin earth. Harvest was impossible. The combines would break apart on the rock every few yards.

Every year, though, Dad planted, and every year we picked rock. The sweat would drip off our noses and amused owls would watch us jump as we uncovered snakes and mice. Our rock piles grew and eventually so did the wheat. It got a little taller and a little more plentiful as each year went by.

The 1960's brought a time of challenge and rebellion even to our isolated family farm. In l967 one of Dad's younger brothers declared that he had had enough of chasing Grandpa around. He'd move out to his own land and be his own boss. He'd raise his family the way he wanted to. He'd dig a well halfway to hell if he had to, but he'd get off that home place and show us all what he could be. Dad ended up digging the well three-quarters of the way to hell for him, and also helped him build his home, which he settled on the south side of Kimama Butte. It was lonely out there, but he was free.

The water well changed things. My dad put in another one, and we went from being tired, sore rock pickers to hot, wet sprinkler pipe movers. The irrigated wheat grew up to my chest and shoulders. It swayed in the Idaho wind like ocean waves. What a crop! What prices for the wheat! The fortune Grandpa had dreamed of was sitting right there in my father's field. Dad would no longer have to own the failures that had never been his to begin with. He put up two new granaries right in the middle of the dilapidated sheep sheds. We shut off the pumps and watched the wheat ripen golden hard.

Meaningful rewards in this tough part of the Northwest are rarely received without some kind of hard sacrifice. But the sacrifice I was about to witness was heart wrenching. It was a hot August afternoon when I heard Grandpa downstairs calling my name. He needed a driver to get him somewhere in a hurry, and he wanted me because I was considered dangerous but fast. His lips were drawn tightly together, and he stared straight ahead without focusing. "What's wrong?" I asked as I got behind the wheel.

"There's a fire on the butte. Get there," was all he said. I flew.

The sky went from hazy to gray and, eventually, to black as we shot closer to our land. We sped over the rough dirt roads. As the car leaped over one mound I saw a huge wall of flame peeling apart the earth and sky. Enormous peaks of orange and red were reaching toward the heavens and devouring our land beneath. We stopped at my uncle's home, and before the dust from the car could settle, his wife came running out to meet us. "It's going to take the house. George went out, but he can't stop it. The wind's bringing it right toward us."

Between their home and the hungry flames stood our beautiful crop, dry and ripe and ready for harvest. But now it would be a vehicle sure to deliver the fire straight to my uncle's back door. As I tried to take in the destructive magnitude of that vast, fiery wall, I saw my father's tractor creeping deliberately along its base. The tractor looked so small that I could barely make out the plow it pulled behind. I saw our tall, heavy wheat deliberately being buried under the powdery soil. My father was making a boundary that the fire could not cross.

The gap became wider and wider between the fire and its golden ripe fuel. Planes quickly came from Twin Falls and dropped foam. Bureau of Land Management trucks came with men and water to drench and beat out what smoldering patches were left. The battle continued into the evening, until finally all that remained was the scorched soil and heavy, gray air. The tractor stopped, and the man who stepped out was not the same person as when he had stepped in. That man, my dad, had plowed under his own success and his own freedom acre by acre. As Grandpa took him home that night, I realized that nothing was free in the Idaho land draw.

Sharon Hutchison, Boise

Wildlife photo opportunities, ranging from the cougars and bighorn sheep of the mountains to the upland game birds and bobcats of the scenic desert areas, are endless.

I enjoy reading American history. The best way to judge the future is by looking at the past. I would want to spend a little time with Chief Joseph, perhaps riding appaloosas together in a quiet river valley somewhere in northern Idaho, where the forests are green and thick and the morning air is often filled with a cooling mist or cold rain.

He would ask me if the white man had been treating his people well, allowing them sufficient room to keep their pride and heritage alive. I would tell him yes.

He would ask me if the wolf and buffalo are still running wild and free in the Idaho territory. I would tell him yes.

Because Chief Joseph is so wise, he would know that I had been answering his questions with lies. But it would break my heart to have to look into the sad eyes of this brave warrior, and speak to him about the reality of today, and the reality of so many of our yesterdays.

Elizabeth Anderson, Boise

The tower of the Morrison-Knudsen Depot is visible from the entire downtown Boise area. The structure houses a historic train museum that is open to the public.

Katherine Albertson Park, in the heart of Boise, emphasizes the charm of natural wildflowers and comfortable walking paths.

A boy offers a friendly touch to horses that feed on the high-country grasses near Salmon.

The famed hot springs area at Burgdorf was a welcome sight for Idaho's early-day miners and fur trappers.

THINGS WERE DIFFERENT

My existence, before transferring to the Northwest from Ohio, consisted of going to work, working, going home from work, falling asleep thinking about work, and working to get up each morning in order to get back to....well, you get the picture. Weekends, too, were spent worrying and studying no-load mutual funds, current inflation factors, and the 7.7% interest rates on a guaranteed investment contract. My soul was being wrung dry by a game that knew no peace....trying to have the most toys when I died. My wife and kids were becoming strangers to me.

This was a common life style in the mid 1970's. It meant putting the family on the back burner. I was investing hard-earned dollars into education, orthodontists, life insurance, and credit cards. I've yet to receive a single dividend check from any of these sources.

I kept telling myself that there would be sufficient time for the little league ball games, walks in the park, building a snowman....tomorrow. But tomorrow never came. What I thought to be a lasting and good marriage soon ran out of gas.

My boss in Ohio, at the time of my zealot career ambitions, was from a state called Idaho, a place, I recalled from geography classes, that was located somewhere south of the Canadian border in the Pacific Northwest....but no one knew or especially cared, about its precise whereabouts. He told me things were different out there. "Travel a few miles in any direction of downtown Boise," he said, "and you could catch enough trout for breakfast any day of the year." After hearing this, my first repugnant thoughts were that of a fishy tasting trout omelette, or a couple of half-cooked rainbows on top of a waffle. I had a great deal to learn.

But true to my boss's word, Idaho has clearly proven over the years to be a state that recommends itself to the stream fisherman who appreciates the feisty pan-fry cutthroat experience, compared to the catfish quantity and relative ease of a "pond" fisherman who uses nightcrawlers and a heavy lead sinker. He explained to me that there was a curious law that caused the fly fishermen and water colorists to gravitate to the states in the Northwest while the pond fishermen and house painters gravitated to the states in the Southwest.

Out of sheer frustration with my personal circumstances, I agreed to the company transfer and bid my family an emotional farewell. My wife, son, and daughter would soon follow me to Idaho, but I was certainly not aware of this at the time.

I remember clearly when my love affair with Idaho began in earnest. Some friends at work had suggested I take my 10-year old son, Justin, who was fast becoming an avid fisherman, to a special place up in the Sawtooth Mountains, a place called Redfish Lake. Before we left, I was given a carefully illustrated map with instructions to get to the gas station in a town called Stanley before they closed for the evening. It was mid October, and if an early snow storm came, you wanted your tank to read FULL. Justin had everything organized in the station wagon when I arrived home from the office. The peanut butter sandwiches that he packed with great care, and placed inside my tackle box, along with the fish hooks and salmon eggs, left a little to be desired, but his sparkle and enthusiasm were contagious.

We headed into the evening on Highway 21, heading north through Idaho City. The serpentine road through the mountains seemed endless. Light needed for safe driving quickly faded. We finally arrived in Stanley, but the night sky was cold and threatening. My friends forgot to mention there'd be a slight difference in the nighttime temperatures between Boise and Stanley. A cowboy bar in town filled the thermos with hot coffee which helped to wash down my peanut butter sandwich. We gassed up the car to read FULL.

Two or three miles from Stanley, our headlights at last located the small wood sign pointing to Redfish. A final mile in the darkness and we sensed we were close to a big lake. We were exhausted and parked the car in a sandy area thick with pine trees. There were no signs of other campers. No lights. No sounds. No campfires. We threw the sleeping bags on the ground and crawled in deeply. I was uneasy about the ice crystals beginning to form on the rocks and patches of grass. We knew not what the morning would bring. I had a sense, however, that with the welcomed sunrise, we might be in for something surprising and perhaps even lovely.

That weekend trip occurred many years ago. Yet I remember that vivid morning as if it happened yesterday. Driven from soreness from sleeping on the frozen ground, and by curiosity, we timidly left the warmth of our sleeping bags to see the first soft light falling on Redfish Lake. Enormous mountains to the south end were crowned with patches of high snow and sculptured layers of gray and purple rock. Half-buried logs and tree stumps protruded from the lake's edges, stained ghost-white from years of water, and sun. Monet, Cezanne, and Van Gogh would have to combine their endless talents on a single canvas to capture the sight our eyes were feasting upon. Thin layers of fog hung over the water, and a green wash of pine trees were reflecting ink-black and bottle green colors. The lake was mirror smooth. Absolutely no sound. Absolutely no motion. Absolutely....beautiful.

A short time later, three men in fishing gear waded quietly into the water from a point where a small stream entered. With our muscles not yet thawed from the long night, we sat in the sun on a boulder and watched the lines from their fly rods move back and forth in slow motion across their shoulders. Yet the lake, the fog, the sky, the trees, and the men fishing, made no noise whatsoever. With this absence of sound, the water and mountains, the company of my young son close to me, I had to turn away for a moment, embarrassed that I may have caught something in my eyes that caused them to moisten just a little. I was quietly proud of my son and overjoyed to be spending time with him again in a state where things, indeed, were different. This was the most beautiful lake I had ever seen or ever dreamed of seeing.

Except for an old and crumpled photograph that's kept in my desk drawer at home, it is all gone now. Years later, when Justin was just 18, he died in a falling accident while working a summer contractor's job in Washington.

Those first early moments at Redfish Lake may have lasted but a short time, but I will always remember them dearly. I may be mistaken, but it seems to me that all the charming and memorable experiences in the world can be quite empty, unless you have a son or daughter or close family member or friend close by to help you share those wonderful little treasures that come around now and then. Those were splendid days.

Robert Shore, Boise

Summer days on Payette Lake provide a slower change of pace. The nights are cool, and the face of nature is simply too beautiful for words to describe.

    My grandparents have a beautiful farm near Soda Springs. I would invite Emily Dickinson to Idaho so that we could share a little supper with them, along with a pot of Grandma's good hot tea.

    To make a prairie it
       takes a clover and one bee,
    And revery.
    The revery alone will do
    If bees are few.

    They love her poetry and would, no doubt, ask Ms. Dickinson about her thoughts on such things as cable TV, Murphy Brown, and desk-top computers. Would she enjoy being able to fax her poetry instantly to any publisher in the world? Both of my grandparents would talk long and hard to her about <u>not</u> changing and updating any of her work so that it might include the latest 20th century terminology.

    To make a prairie it
       takes a clover and one bee,
    And one wide-screened TV
    The wide-screened TV will do
    If bees are few.

Jennifer Brooks, Pocatello

FIRST IDAHO RAINBOW

The summer of 1950 was hot and humid in Peoria, Illinois. The Illinois River ran sluggish and dirty through the city. I crossed it daily on the way to by job at the Caterpillar Tractor Company. I tossed and turned on my bed in the stifling night heat thinking of my upcoming trip to the west.

I was looking forward to the annual factory shutdown during the first two weeks of August for inventory and vacations. A skeleton crew stayed on to take inventory and all others had their two weeks of vacation.

I had heard much conversation from some friends who had vacationed in the west. They had told of the cool, dry air, beautiful mountains, and trout-filled lakes. They told of sparkling, rushing, ice-cold streams that ran all summer long and were clean enough to drink from. I had to experience this myself.

Couldn't wait to get started. I was single and 20 years old. My dad and younger brother were making the trip with me. Mother could not come because of the needs of her aging parents.

Our long thought-out plan was to travel across the states of Missouri, Kansas, Colorado, Wyoming, Idaho, and Oregon, and then circle down into California and take a southern route back home to Harrisburg, Illinois.

We arrived in Boise late on the evening of August 2, 1950, and proceeded on to Homedale to locate a cousin who had started a welding/blacksmith shop there. He had worked for six years at the Bradley Mining Company in Stibnite, Idaho. The next day he said that he wanted to show us some pretty country.

We drove up the winding ponderosa-lined road to Cascade, along the rushing Payette River, and proceeded past Warm Lake and Big Creek summit, through Yellow Pine to the still busy mining town of Stibnite. It was an awesome trip for a midwesterner. We stopped at the "Ice Hole" near Yellow Pine and stopped and took a short swim at Warm Lake. The ore trucks were still hauling ore to Cascade for shipment. I almost smashed head-on with one on a tight turn. It taught me to be much more cautious and alert.

We hiked into a small, high-mountain lake and spent the night camping. I caught my first rainbow trout. What a fish! What a memory! I was awestruck with the beauty of everything. And I couldn't believe that air could look and smell so clean. The moon looked close enough to touch. It was almost a spiritual experience. I was hooked!

The next few days were a revelation. How could you possibly need your car heater and a warm coat to go to work in the morning, only to drive home in 85-degree heat in the afternoon, and then sleep under a thick blanket at night? I couldn't believe it. I loved it!

I mustered my courage and announced to my dad and brother that I was staying in Idaho, and, since it was my car, they would have to stay or find other transportation home. They elected to take the train back to Illinois while I remained in Idaho.

The Korean War was heating up and I was draft age. I joined the Idaho Air National Guard, and almost immediately our unit was called to active duty and sent to Moody Air Force Base in Valdosta, Georgia.

We spent time in Georgia and eventually were sent to George Air Force Base in Victorville, California. But I never forgot beautiful Idaho. When I was discharged I made a short visit back to Illinois, but within months I was back in the hills of Idaho....this time to stay.

It's been 42 years now. I have made many trips back to the Midwest to visit relatives and friends. It is lovely there in the autumn. However, I have never been tempted to return there to live. I married an Idaho girl and raised my family here. I would do it all over again without hesitation, without even blinking an eye.

Idaho may not be the best place in the world to make a living, but it has to be among the best places in the world to live and raise your children.

Jim Hancock, Boise

THE VIEW FROM THE STATION

It was one o'clock in the morning in June 1983 when our Amtrak train pulled into the Boise station. My family and I were on our last venture of our business/pleasure trip through the Northwest from our home in Dayton, Ohio.

A colleague of my husband from the Veterans Medical Center in Dayton had suggested if we really desired a job relocation that he visit and make a personal contact with all Veterans Administration hospital directors from Washington to northern California and back through the Pacific Northwest. That sounded like a great idea!

Nineteen hundred miles from home, and nearing the conclusion of our journey, we stepped off into the crystal-clear morning air and sat on the grass outside the Amtrak station overlooking the city of Boise. The picture-perfect city imprinted in our minds will forever be remembered. The street lights aglow lined Capitol Boulevard to the distant end where we could see the state capitol building silhouetted by massive trees and mountains. The lights circling the majestic dome had represented the true center of Idaho. What a breathtaking sight, we all thought! Without hesitation, and midst the quietness of the moment, I spoke with affirmation to my family, "You can all go back to Ohio, I'm staying right here!"

The Ohio Valley area had been our home for the past eight years. Progressively we had grown tired and weary of the crowds of people, severe summer humidity, and the shocking crime rates, to say nothing about the difficult winters. We soon fell out of love with Ohio and IN LOVE with Idaho.

Two days sightseeing around the Treasure Valley convinced us all that Boise, Idaho, was our choice for a new home, a new VA assignment, and, hopefully, retirement for the future. The beauty of the mountains, the cleanliness of the city itself, and the incredible peacefulness of a smaller community made an indelible imprint on our minds.

We were told an approaching vacancy was soon to be available at the Boise Veterans Medical Center. Our dream and vision of returning, however, was not realized until a few years later, in 1987. Though it took four years to see those hopes and desires come true, our prayers were never lessened by the thought that someday we would return to the lovely and proud City of Trees and the memory we all had so vividly of that charming, crystal-clear morning, four years earlier, as we sat together on the grass at the Boise train station some 1,900 miles from our home in Ohio.

Winifred L. Wallace, Boise

Priest Lake, in Idaho's northern panhandle, is remote and deserted, even on a warm summer day. The tree-shaded banks provide quiet fishing camps.

Spring and summer flowers surround Idaho's state capitol building, completed in the year 1920.

Following the exchange of wedding vows, a young couple enjoys the view from a mountaintop at Seven Devils, above Riggins.

A weathered face from a totem pole near Sun Valley.

A cold stream in the pristine wilderness area of the White Cloud Mountains beckons experienced cross-country skiers.

Prospectors and miners have left rusted ore wagons near the historical ghost towns near Sunbeam.

On a sunny afternoon, I would like to walk the deserted streets of Silver City with Mark Twain. Would the nineteenth-century architecture remind him of some old "jumping frog" stories from his days in Virginia City, Nevada? How would he describe this old mining town surrounded with the colorful hills and narrow roads? It would be interesting to hear his comments after he had read the latest Sunday issue of The Idaho Statesman. What would he think of the volume of advertising? What would he think of "Calvin & Hobbes" and "The Far Side?"

Christine Doerr, Boise

AUNT KATE

To some of the younger people today, World War II is an ancient chapter in our history, in which you can only understand its significance by reading about it or by watching old black and white movies on late night TV. But to those who experienced those unforgettable years in the early 1940's, the memories are clear as the wind and bright as the noonday sun.

My name is Irene, and I was born in London, England. I had a very sweet and kind Aunt Kate, and whenever she visited us in London she would sit me on her lap and sing to me.

Two very special songs we sang were called "Away Beyond the Hills of Idaho" and "I Want To Go To Idaho". This first song, I think, is pretty well known, but I have never met anyone who knows or has heard of the second one. All I can remember of it is, "I want to go to Idaho, so hurry along, hurry along." Of course, as a child and as a young girl, I had no idea where Idaho was but it sounded like some place very beautiful and magical to me.

As the years went by, I always had those two very special tunes tucked away in the back of my mind, and from time to time I would sing and hum them to myself. Often, I would think about the words and how lovely this place must be. It sounded like some far-off magic paradise. Now I know there is a "real" Idaho, and I recall when I was a youngster in England that I would occasionally daydream about a nice boy who might be living there in those hills and who might just happen to like me. But then, it's only a song....beautiful thoughts were to be put away like treasured gifts.

But the time now is 1944. I have just completed the military driving school in the mountainous country of north Wales, during what they said was one of the worst winters in England's history. I became a good driver, however, and I loved all aspects of it and enjoyed being out driving army trucks of all nationalities, all over Britain. As convoy drivers and young ladies, we belonged to the Royal Army Ordnance Corps that had to supply the whole army with much needed transportation vehicles such as trucks, cars, tanks, etc. Our military camp for 35 drivers was a beautiful old English stone house, something like a small castle set in the green, quiet countryside of Wiltshire, and we called it "home". Near our castle home sat a huge Royal Air Force Stirling Bomber aircraft, with four huge engines and wings that seemed to stretch out forever. There were many times when we would be driven home in one of those military trucks, tired and sleepy, and we would often see our bomber with wings out stretched, just like a big welcome home sign. We all had tears in our eyes when the R.A.F. came to fly her out for duty.

It is now a cold Christmas morning in London in 1944, and all of us are off-duty and running around in our blue and white striped army pajamas, enjoying the haunting music of Bing Crosby singing "White Christmas", and I remember us chatting and laughing and telling crazy stories of our days out on convoys. But our officer came in shortly and asked if someone would take 35 meat plates and 35 sweet plates to the men's cookhouse, as we were all eating Christmas dinner together that year. Since we were having such a good time, everyone seemed reluctant to to do this errand. The female officer then looked straight at me and asked if I would go. I said, "Yes," although I really didn't want to leave the other girls on that Christmas holiday.

I jumped into the nearest truck that was in the court yard and drove out into a soft, falling snow to a town called Malmesbury, three miles down the road. I had only gone about one mile when a plume of water shot up like a cannon through the hole in my truck's radiator cap. I slowed to a stop right outside a charming English pub which had thick snow on the roof and a comforting orange glow in its Tudor style windows. A happy sight to me. That's when it happened.

I got out of the truck and walked a little pathway to the old oak door and gently knocked a couple of times. I waited a long time, but then the door opened and there stood the most handsome man I had ever seen, six foot two, a tec sergeant in the U.S. Army, and he smiled at me and he had the most beautiful white teeth when he smiled. I was so surprised, I didn't know what to say, but a little voice in the back of my head said, "That's going to be your husband".

I finally pulled myself together enough to ask if I could have some water for my truck. He said, "Yes, certainly. I'll get it for you." He came back with water and we walked to truck and he felt the engine and said it was frozen up. I told him about my food plates and he said, "Don't worry. We will take you to your destination because you can't drive your truck the way it is." This handsome gentleman-sergeant invited me to come in to have something warm to drink next to the stove. I went in and we joined another officer or two and sat down and I chatted a little bit with them. I didn't drink before, so the combination of the brandy and this handsome officer made me a little dizzy.

I almost forgot what I was sent to do! The kind sergeant steered me to their car, an old English car with U.S.A. license plates, and he carefully placed me in the back seat with my 70 food plates. The two-mile journey was icy, and we fishtailed most of the way. But I was too happy to be scared. Upon arriving at men's cookhouse, the car began to slide and we hit part of the building, which brought out the chefs to see what was going on.

The English chefs invited my two American friends in to enjoy Christmas dinner with them, but they couldn't stay. A short time later, however, the chefs came out and offered them each a hot steaming turkey leg. I thanked them very much for the help and the ride, and they waved goodbye to me, both smiling as they disappeared down the road. For days I couldn't think of anything else but that handsome U.S. Sergeant. He seemed exactly the right kind of person for me, but I didn't think I would ever, ever see him again.

But one evening, while I was at an English dance talking to some of the girls, in comes this charming man with his beautiful smile and he sits right down beside me. I was so delighted and happy to see him again, but I wondered, "How could such a nice man like that ever want to see me again?" After all, I was always in dull army uniform: pants, boots, and battle top (like Eisenhower jackets). How could a girl look attractive without pretty clothes? Anyway, he said he had been "looking for me all over". Naturally, my friends were very impressed and later said, "Where in the world did you find such a good looking man?"

From that point he said he would be right in the town square where we were stationed and he then helped me down from truck and we went to a little corner cafe and drank some hot tea and talked, and talked, and talked. It was at that moment when I asked him where he was from and he said a place called "Idaho." I almost fainted! I then asked if he lived in the "Hills of Idaho," and he said, "Yes, ma'am."

Time drifted by, and one day, long after the war had ended, I boarded the *Queen Mary* to come to this mysterious land called Idaho. I married that nice sergeant, and we have a very handsome son, just like his dad, who is, by the way, a former tec sergeant of 120th General Hospital. I have been in the land of magic for 38 years now, and I still love the Idaho hills, the mountains, the people, and all Idaho. My husband is in heaven now, but our son who is well-traveled has often said, "There is no place in the world more beautiful than Idaho." I have thought that since being a very young girl back in England when my Aunt Kate and I sang those lovely songs.

Thank you Aunt Kate. Thank you Idaho.

                                        Irene Lackey, Juliaetta

Rivers of cold white water invite kayakers and rafters to the ultimate summer adventure.

John Lennon. Without question. If I could bring just one person back from the dead to visit with me in Idaho, that one person would have to be John Lennon, the best of the Beatles.

I would take him to the Fiddlers Contest over in Weiser and then drive up to Yellow Pine with him for the Harmonica Festival. They would love him in Weiser. They would love him in Yellow Pine. They would love John anywhere in Idaho. I would introduce him to a few of my friends in Kamiah.

Jack Barnes, Kamiah

Cattle slumber in the cool air near the Sawtooth Mountains. Abundant winter snows provide the cattle with rich, green summer pastures.

Glass jars in a window await Mom's homegrown fruits and vegetables.

The McCall Winter Carnival also features parades, cross-country skiing, and snowmobile races.

The picturesque town of McCall receives visitors from all parts of the country during its annual ice sculpture contest.

A Kodacolor smile from a young parade participant.

GIFT-WRAPPED

More than 30 years ago my 13 year old daughter and I were driving through Boise on our way back to Seattle. We had just returned from a vacation trip to Yellowstone Park. It was late afternoon and as we headed west through the then sparsely populated suburbs, the sun was gilding grain fields with its last golden rays and there was a lovely violet band around the horizon. When I exclaimed at the beauty of the desert evening and the radiance of the setting sun, my daughter said: "Mom, it looks like God has gift-wrapped the world."

Many years later, when that same daughter, along with her husband and two young children had an opportunity to better themselves economically by moving to Boise, I decided I would like to tag along. As a widowed older woman, my alternatives were to stay where I was among dear but aging friends, or, to move to Boise. Although I had lived in California earlier in my life and loved it, that was before it became wall-to-wall suburbs, wall-to-wall people. After making several interesting trips to Idaho to visit my family, and to check out a few of the amenities, my choice became wonderfully clear to me.

At the time when I moved chattels and cat to Boise, the downtown area was no-man's land and the winter skies were sometimes hazy, but there was all that bounteous space in which to live! Miles and miles and miles of space, most of it charming and beautiful. And those sunsets!

But now, the world has discovered my secret Shangri-la in the Pacific Northwest. A revitalized Boise is drawing so many newcomers here that I am inclined to feel like joining some of those real old-timers in complaining about the lack of elbow room. But someone did make room for me when I first arrived here, and I can sympathetically understand the attraction this part of the country has for those seeking a better life. Then too, maybe "God's gift-wrapped package" got to them as well.

Elinor M. Thomas, Boise

One of the sweet amenities to living in Idaho is our availability to so many lovely parts of the country that are located in the adjoining states like Oregon, Washington, Montana and Wyoming. Thomas Jefferson devoted almost 10 years of his life in seeing that the unknown territory in the Pacific Northwest was secured and intelligently explored by the United States. Part of that $15,000,000 Louisiana Purchase included the land we now call Idaho. Wouldn't it be wonderful to accompany Mr. Jefferson today as he toured some of the beautiful and interesting parts of the Northwest?

Mr. Jefferson would, in all probability, choose Idaho to be his home in the Northwest, not just because of the spirit of the freedom loving compatriots who live here, but because it would be so centrally located for some long exploratory weekends. He'd probably start by building a mini-Monticello type condo in a town like McCall, Idaho.

From McCall, he could easily helicopter over to the Columbia Gorge to see the plunging waterfalls, the unique flowers and wildlife, that his two devoted friends, Lewis and Clark, wrote to him about on their historic mission to the Pacific in 1805. Jefferson would then, perhaps, pick up a rental car in Portland and drive down to Astoria and visit the Northwest's beautiful coastline, dotted with charming places called Yachats and Cannon Beach, Manzanita and Coos Bay, Hoquiam and Chinook.

Being something of a gentleman farmer, he would want to investigate and taste the grapes and apples grown in the Hood River Valley that burst with incomparable flavor each summer.

I would hope that Mr. Jefferson would then head a little north to enjoy a bit of the high country of the Olympic Peninsula and the rain forests of Hoh Valley in Washington, and perhaps even "do lunch" at the Space Needle in Seattle.

Next he would head east. He would want to see for himself the sophisticated machinery used to harvest the fruits and vegetables of the Columbia Basin and the golden wheat fields of the Palouse country. And being a scientist, Thomas Jefferson would want to spend a little time probing the glacier areas of northern Montana.

And life, of course, never ceases to fascinate visitors to the Yellowstone area of Wyoming. What, in God's name, would he say after witnessing some of the miracles of Yellowstone, the acres of spectacular clouds of steaming geysers, the 300-foot cascading waterfalls of the Yellowstone River, and the majestic mountain peaks of the Tetons?

Granted, his discerning eye for detail and his inquisitive mind would eventually lead Mr. Jefferson to ask a few sensitive questions. Questions concerning the logging and employment problems, the spotted owl. Questions concerning the high powered dams situated on the rivers throughout the Northwest. He would want to know how the salmon are able to negotiate such obstacles while on their way home to spawn.

Oh, to have the personal thoughts and input of this sagacious gentleman from Virginia. The awesome light that he would shine on us as we head towards the precipitous 21st century.

James McFadden, Meridian

FIVE ACRE FARM

I rode into Idaho on my suitcase in the summer of 1945. The wheels that propelled my luggage west clicked off the miles on a train track across the Wyoming prairie. I sat on my suitcase in the aisle of the train with other civilians, because all the seats in the coach were occupied by servicemen bound for the West Coast. Sometime in the long night ride, a young G. I. offered to let me sit on his lap for a while, but my mother vetoed the plan; it wouldn't be proper, she said, for a 12 year old girl to sit on the lap of a soldier in the dark, even if he was sworn by the government of the United States to protect and defend her.

A year earlier, 1944, our family of four had traveled in the opposite direction, east to Missouri. At that time we rode in a tarpaulin-covered truck loaded with all our possessions: a piano, pots and pans, pillows and pictures. I sat in the back of the truck and held my cat on my lap. I watched the rain drizzle off the canvas overhead and wondered if we would ever have a real home, ever settle down in "one place" and stay there.

We didn't stay in Missouri. After a nightmare year of tornadoes and ice storms, chiggers, snakes and crawdads and people who talked "funny." ("Git yer toggin on....let's traipse," they said, "an we'll carry ye over to town.") We "carried" ourselves to the train station and left, headed back to the West.

This time, however, we traveled lighter, much lighter; my parents sold the piano, the pots and pans and pillows....just about everything was gone but the priceless family pictures. What was left we stuffed into four suitcases and a packing box and loaded them and ourselves on a train bound for Idaho.

Why Idaho? Because in 1936 my grandparents gave up on the wind and grasshoppers of Wyoming and moved here to pick fruit. They wanted us to join them. The first summer we visited them we picked fruit, too. My mother canned a hundred quarts of cherries and peaches and shipped them all back to Wyoming. She also entered a few jars in the county fair. The cherries won a blue ribbon; they were so large the judges mistook them for plums.

By the time we stepped off the train in Payette, Idaho, in 1945, along with a lot of soldiers and sailors, my grandparents had bought a little farm, five acres, about a mile from town. My grandfather milked three cows and tended a small prune orchard. Grandmother raised a garden and Austra-White chickens. They sold the milk and eggs to the creamery and the prunes to the fruit packer. We moved in with them and helped with the daily chores.

My first impression of this new land was that it had more trees and water than I had ever seen. And the wind didn't blow day and night, the way it did in Wyoming. Once in a while a little dust storm carrying a few drops of rain would blow upon on a hot summer evening, but it was over in minutes. "An Oregon mist," my grandmother called the squall. "Missed Oregon....hit Idaho."

On Sunday afternoons, all six of us, my grandparents and our family of four, squeezed into Grandpa's black '36 Chevy with the scratchy seat covers and no air-conditioner, and we toured the valley. We drove to Fruitland and New Plymouth, Parma and Notus. Sometimes we even crossed the Snake River to Ontario and Vale. My dad and grandfather sat in the front seat and appraised other farmers' fields of potatoes and corn, and they talked about buying us a little farm, just as if we could afford such a prize. But, of course, it didn't cost anything to dream. And we did lots of dreamin' in that old Chevy.

My dad never did get his little farm in Idaho. In the fall of 1946 he went to work for Morrison-Knudsen and we moved to a tiny basement apartment on Hill Road near Boise. The foothills above Hill Road were unpopulated then; they were our playground. On school days we walked down to State Street to catch the bus that took us to North Junior High. It wasn't called "North" then, because it was the only junior high school in the city.

I remember the Saturdays when my mother and sister and I dressed up in our better clothes and went downtown to shop at the Bon Marche or to appointments with dentists or doctors in the Eastman Building. Then we'd have lunch in the Mode tearoom and stroll through the lobby of the Hotel Boise. People in idle conversation remarked how fast the city was growing...why, someday they wouldn't be surprised to see Boise's population reach as high as 50,000.

Boise and all of Idaho has grown since it became my home 47 years ago. Small family orchards have disappeared, replaced by large, sophisticated-looking fields of sugar beets, onions, and mint. A farmer can't make a living on five acres anymore, the way my grandfather did. Many small farms like his have been swallowed up in urban sprawl, the land converted to acres of houses occupied by newcomers. We are rapidly becoming cosmopolitan; we have enough traffic for smog now. Yet, in Boise, cows still graze in pastures abutting the state's largest shopping mall.

Last year I attended a wedding in California where I met a couple of men from Atlanta, Georgia. They barely concealed their Southern superiority when I told them I lived in Idaho. "However do people LIVE in Idaho?" one of them drawled.

"Very well," I replied. "We have commerce and industry and tourism. We're not all poor 'dirt farmers'. Did you know there are more millionaires per capita in Idaho than there are in any other state?"

They didn't. But as they turned away I heard one snicker, "Just how many millionaires do you suppose that might be....three?"

I remember being offended by his remark, but maybe there was more truth to it than he supposed. Lately I've observed that just about every other park, construction company, feed lot and fertilizer plant, stadium, public building, cultural academy, college, and performing arts center in the Boise Valley bears the name of three particular individuals: Albertson, Morrison, or Simplot.

At times these wealthy Idaho benefactors must wring their hands in dismay when they realize just how little their enormous generosity in time and money has accomplished in sophisticating the rest of us Idahoans. A stroll around town any day of the week, for example, clearly reveals that most Idahoans prefer to express themselves through bumper stickers and graffiti T-shirts rather than through the media of beautiful art and music. People who otherwise appear inarticulate speak out on their clothes and the bumper stickers on their cars and pick-ups.

In the mall the T-shirt on a young boy admonishes, "Button Your Fly." A frowsy teenager looking for trouble sports instructions on her chest, "In Case Of Rape....This Side Up." A pair of retirees in look-alike shirts identify themselves: "Old Fart" and "Old Fart's Wife."

A car passes near by. "Life Is Hell....Then You Die" is the dire pronouncement on its bumper. Further down the street the message on another disenchanted driver's car bemoans her financial status: "I'm So Broke I Can't Even Pay Attention!" A mud-spattered pickup truck with mandatory gun rack and big sheep dog in the back turns the corner. "Eat Lamb," its bumper sticker coaxes, "50,000 coyotes can't be wrong".

If the expression, "It takes all kinds..." is true, Idahoans affirm it. The same state that is home to the T-shirt and bumper sticker crowd has also sheltered those of greater literary stature: Ezra Pound, Ernest Hemingway, Vardis Fisher, and Patrick McManus. We are indeed unique in our diversity, yet bound together by one philosophy.... our loyalty to the proud and beautiful state that took us in.

Idaho is a conglomeration of immigrants. We older transplants are like the Joads in *The Grapes Of Wrath*. Burned out, blown out and starved out in Kansas, Missouri, Oklahoma, Colorado, and Illinois, we crammed what was left of our little bit of life into packing crates and tin suitcases and headed for the promised land. We found it when we entered Idaho. Today, another generation migrates here, seeking relief from other disasters: earthquakes, pollution, crime, and gangs, or they are hard working people forced to live in poverty. They come looking for a safer place for their kids, a saner lifestyle for themselves. They find these things in Idaho.

This state has taken very good care of a lot of us immigrants. For me it brought me a husband, blown here on the dust of a Colorado drought. Idaho educated our children so well that they left us for wonderful paying jobs elsewhere. Now in retirement, we travel to other places to see what we've missed....and find nothing. We've had it all right here, all the time.

Outsiders may criticize our "tater" license plates and narrow roads, but they would be hard pressed to find fault with the things here that really matter: gracefully colored foothills, mountains and rivers, incredibly blue skies, glorious sunsets, and four mild seasons.... each season distinctive, each season breathtaking.

One morning this summer, I leaned on a log fence in Ponderosa Park near McCall and looked across the water of Payette Lake. A sailboat passed by, a large white pearl on a blue velvet sea. Near the shore an osprey dove into the shallow water and snatched an unwary fish. A few yards away a gray squirrel peeled long-green needles from a sticky pine cone, then scurried to a puddle to wash the bitter pitch from its mouth. There was a small deer that moved down the path to the beach. Earlier that same morning there was a skinny red fox running through huckleberry bushes in search of breakfast.

I would rather be here than anywhere else on this earth.

Lynn Farley, Boise

Sheep that graze near Soldier Mountain are at ease, knowing the Basque sheepherders and their dogs are devoted to their protection.

A flower-strewn mailbox near Riggins offers a pastoral setting for the mailman.

Is there a better place anywhere in the country to raise a family? Many parents who have moved to Idaho from other parts of the U.S.A. think not.

Last evening light on a sunflower.

When it comes to caring and support of wild birds of prey, Idahoans are committed for the long haul. Sanctuaries, highly trained experts, and financial backing provide much-needed assistance to eagles and falcons.

A quiet, sleepy Stanley Lake.

Mom and her young colt share a crisp summer morning together near Boise.

When composer Aaron Copeland wrote his Appalachian Spring symphony, he spoke of the long walks he took on the trails high in the Blue Ridge Mountains, visiting the small towns and the people who had to work so very hard to survive the long, tough winters. But the incomparable spring that always came in April and May would bring life, color, and warmth to Appalachia, and this was the inspiration for his music.

I would like to introduce Aaron Copeland to the Palouse country, situated in the northern panhandle of Idaho. The top soil in Palouse country is deep and rich and dark. It produces fields of golden wheat like no other parts of the world. These Idahoans are honest and hard working. Rows of giant combines can be seen miles away in the distance, slowly crawling across the rolling plateaus of brown, yellow, and golden fields. The farm homes are picture-book beautiful, and grain storage towers seem to rise to the clouds like cathedrals.

Copeland would be awe-inspired with its beauty. And, oh, what music he would compose. The homemade jellies and thick-crusted breads and fruit pies these Palouse women prepare in their kitchens would inspire even a Bach or a Beethoven to greater things. I adore this country and the splendid people who live there.

C. R. Overman, Moscow

A GUTSY KID

One particular Idaho experience, which has remained in my memory over the years, occurred in 1976. But first, allow me to give you some background.

I remember my childhood in Cincinnati as being extremely happy and secure. My father and I were close friends but he died of leukemia when I was 10 and my world suddenly became lonely and confusing. My mother tried her best to be two parents for me, but it was difficult for her to understand and talk about the really serious and important things in life: how to throw a curve ball, for example, and the best way to break up a double play when sliding into second base, or when to swing for the fences when the tying runner was on third. She could see that the loss of my father hurt terribly, and she acted quickly to try and fill the void. One day she introduced me to a guy named David.

Dave said he was a catcher with a semi-pro ball club, and he was looking for someone who might help him get ready for the spring tryouts. He wanted to know if I knew of someone who could throw him a few pitches. He had a catcher's mitt that would make my pitches sound like cracks from a cannon. I was impressed.

This was the beginning of an important friendship in my young life. Granted, he wasn't my dad, but it was like having a big brother. I could even talk to him about illegal spit balls without having to worry about getting a lecture from Mom on the high moral fortitude necessary for good sportsmanship.

It was in large part the example of Dave that I became involved with the Big Brothers and Sisters program when I was in college. And years later, when my business resulted in my move to Boise, I wasted little time in offering my time as a volunteer. It was my involvement with a little brother out here that I first began to understand something. Idaho, and the people who lived in Idaho, were special. For example, take what happened to me and my first little brother, whose name was Todd.

Todd was the oldest of four children and he was already 14 when his mother approached the Big Brothers and Sisters program. The father had deserted the family two years earlier. There was no way the mother was able to influence Todd's behavior. He would often skip school and would hitchhike rides to other towns with no money or food in his pockets. His attempts at getting something to eat and finding a place to sleep inevitably led to problems with the local police.

Todd's explanations were always the same. He simply wanted to get a job somewhere and be able to help provide some money for the family. He was wasting his time in school. The people at Big Brothers and Sisters called me and asked if I would be interested in helping.

Writing about this so many years later, it is difficult to sort out the exact chain of events that led to Todd and I becoming good friends. But I recall that we had one common interest and that was the strong desire to go deer hunting someday. Todd did not have a rifle but I had two friends at work , Mike and Woody, who invited me to go hunting with them when the season opened in a few weeks. They had an extra gun and said my little brother would simply make the trip extra-enjoyable.

We spent several afternoons over at Woody's farm practicing shooting and sighting in our rifles. A person doesn't have to be particularly observant to realize that many Idahoans have a strong inner magnet that draws them to the woods and farthest parts of the hills and valleys when autumn arrives, especially when deer and elk season opens. And it is probably unnecessary to point out to Idaho residents that from about the first week in August, hunters are already making serious plans and look forward with gusto to the time when the summer tourists leave, the aspens turn yellow, and the 30.06 Winchesters and full and modified

Springfields with Leupold scopes come down from the walls. In order to understand the affection they have for their weapons, you would have to appreciate the intense love and feelings a panda bear has for its first-born cubs.

At last, opening day arrived. Todd and I left on a Saturday morning, long before sunrise. We met Mike and Woody at a place on the far side of Anderson Ranch Dam where they had a campsite. They had spent the previous day up in the hills checking for recent signs and evidence of deer tracks. My little brother enthusiastically helped out by chopping wood and doing the dishes following a campfire breakfast of thick bacon slices with homemade cinnamon roles. Our excitement could be bottled up no longer. It was time to hunt.

The area around Trinity Lakes is a beautiful place to hunt, doubly so when the sun is bright and gives off a little warmth. Just the simple experience of being high in the mountains, listening, seeing, feeling the wind, was reward enough for me. But Woody and Mike were determined to allow young Todd to have at least one good shot at a buck on his first hunting trip. Their own deer hunting techniques originated from a finely honed tradition dating back to when they were both young boys living in small towns in eastern Idaho when the kill was, if fact, important table fare. One deer would lay in a good supply of winter meat for the family.

Because the weather was dry and other hunters would be scaring up the deer, causing them to move about chaotically, Mike thought it best to place Todd and myself together in an area of heavy boulders where we could hide ourselves in thick overhanging branches. They, on the other hand, would circle from the bottom of a steep slope, and try to drive any deer in the area, right up and into our gun sights.

Mike and Woody checked their compasses and the sun and threw dead grass into the air to check the direction of the wind. They both quietly disappeared into the trees. The ground was filled with dry leaves and broken limbs, yet you could not hear the slightest sound of their movements through the woods.

Approximately an hour later, we heard them communicating with each other by making bird calls and whistles. That's when it happened.

Just 40 yards away, a buck's head appeared before us. Half its body was hidden from view by trees, but the head and antlers were huge and the sun shone on his face through the forest shadows like a Hollywood spotlight. I think I can say without contradiction that any one of the four of us could easily have pulled the trigger on him right then and there. Through our gun sights, we could see that this stately whitetail was fat and would be wonderfully flavored for many enjoyable meals to come. We had him surrounded on all sides with four 30.06s. At this point, we couldn't lose. Or could we?

We waited for Todd to take the first shot. The deer now appeared nervous and his instincts were making his eyes and head dart in all directions. Then the deer froze....like a statue. We could practically taste the venison steaks, cooked slowly outdoors over hot coals, lightly seasoned with cracked pepper and mushrooms. Why wouldn't Todd fire? He had the animal in his sights for over a half minute. His rifle began to quiver. His forehead was wet with perspiration. Todd blinked his eyes a couple of times and slowly raised his gun toward the blue sky and pulled the trigger. The shot echoed through the hills. The deer bolted like lightning and thunder down the side of that mountain, crashing into shrubs and knocking over anything in its way. He was gone. He was history.

In a few hours we would all have to break camp and head back to Boise. This opportunity to fell a three or four-point buck slipped through our hands like quicksilver, a traumatic disappointment. But a couple of things happened that day to make that trip not only enjoyable, but unforgettable.

The first thing was a spectacular shot by Woody on our drive back down the mountain. He brought down a fat sage hen from a high tree with one perfect shot. Back at camp, he plucked the bird and prepared a stew that included potatoes, carrots, and onions. It would simmer for hours in the ground with hot coals from the fire. Our appetites were ravenous. The stew, served with hot coffee around the campfire, was wonderful.

And secondly, my little brother finally opened up and began to talk to us apologetically about his reasons for allowing the whitetail to escape. He said that the deer was looking at him right in the eyes. "His eyes were beautiful. He looked so proud. It was the most beautiful thing I've ever seen. I couldn't kill him and I didn't want anyone else to kill him. I just wanted him to have a fair chance."

The sight of a beautiful animal through a gun sight conjures up many different emotions in different people. But a gutsy Idaho kid, just 14 years old, learned something about himself that day and how he felt about killing big game. Its been over 12 years now since I've been in touch with Todd, but should he ever happen to read this story about our trip to the Trinity Lakes, I hope he realizes how much all of us respected his courage, and his decision....to give that deer his freedom. Woody, Mike, and I learned a great deal from you that day.

Walter Wells, Boise

THE COLOR IN THE THREADS

The tapestry of life weaves contrasting threads that seem to have no connection to the picture as a whole. Rather, they add a single splash of color and then seem to disappear. But if you follow that single thread, it weaves itself into a new picture where it is the central theme.

The single thread that ties my life to Idaho zoomed across the tapestry in the mid-1950's. My early memories of Idaho are childlike in their simplicity. A long journey ("Are we almost there?"). Miles and miles of endless green fields. Grey skies that promise snow but do not materialize. Hot springs swimming. The long trip was a holiday visit to an aunt that lived in Idaho. The boredom of the travel and the high spot of the swimming are retained in memory 40 years later.

The thread and color gather strength in 1977 as my husband's parents move to New Plymouth, Idaho. The mountains remind them of their last home in Colorado, the Bookcliffs near Grand Junction. Also, they say the fishing will be better for an avid fishing father. The threads make larger splashes now as visits are remembered.

In 1986, the parents are growing old. It is time for someone to care for them. The single thread now becomes the central color as Idaho becomes the new residence.

First images and impressions here are of a slow-paced civilization where neighbor knows and cares for neighbor. Some of the big city lights are missing, but then so are some of the big city fights.

A mother dies. A father becomes dependent and dies. A child matures and marries. The color gathers and spreads. Another mother cries for aid. A grandchild is born. Another father dies. The color dominates and recedes.

Population increases. The big city lights are here. The big city fights are here. But, the color is the master of the tapestry. The roots grow deep. The sun shines. Life moves forward.

Idaho is home.

Alice M. Armstrong, Nampa

Personal note: Proceeds from the sale of this book are being donated to the wild birds of prey organizations in Idaho. This unique part of the Northwest has an enormous untapped potential for assisting the endangered falcons, hawks, and eagles. Because of the hard work and devoted backing of a few, these projects are, at long last, beginning to be realized for their success and importance. The only restrictions on the further achievements of these people is our failure to understand the serious need for more volunteers and financial support. Your continued involvement is needed and appreciated. Thank you.

Walter Wells